TODAY'S MORNING VOCABULARY

Yoo Heekyung

Translated from Korean by
Stine An

ZEPHYR PRESS

First published in Korea as 오늘 아침 단어
by Moonji Publishing Co., Ltd

Published in agreement with Nasun Agency

Book design by typeslowly

Today's Morning Vocabulary is published with the support of the Literature Translation Institute of Korea (LTI Korea). Zephyr Press also acknowledges with gratitude the financial support of the Massachusetts Cultural Council and the Academy of American Poets with funds from the Amazon Literary Partnership Poetry Fund.

LTI LITERATURE TRANSLATION INSTITUTE OF KOREA

Mass Cultural Council

Zephyr Press, a non-profit arts and education 501(c)(3) organization, publishes literary titles that foster a deeper understanding of cultures and languages. Zephyr Press books are distributed to the trade by Consortium Book Sales and Distribution [www.cbsd.com].

Cataloging-in-publication data is available from the Library of Congress.

ISBN 978-1938890-29-1

ZEPHYR PRESS
www.zephyrpress.org

Table of Contents

PART II

PART III

Dedication

To my mother

Note from the poet

Searching for dozens of words and a single person at the same time—I am still attending to this work.

June 2011, Yoo Heekyung

PART I

in dreams

the sleeping things took to the streets
the long sleeves folded back their sleeves

the window pane remained fogged with breath
the burning field refused to go out
the wind kept rising up and up
and the footsteps were still wandering

only the heart bore a single sigh
and someone cried through the whole night

i held my being softly
i beheld my cradled self
a bright light glowed
the rest remained in darkness

and so my howl-like self
became an empty bell

when i put my neck inside a t-shirt i think

1

when i put my neck inside a t-shirt i think
it's cramped in here and i don't know you
on the kitchen table several bills are laid to rest
mother scrubs her afterimage like a dish
i'm decorated onto one side of the wall
a morning that shrinks the veins of sycamore leaves
sharpened toward myself and in several pieces
can i possibly call something like this threadbare?

2

when i put my neck inside a t-shirt i think
while shaving i cut the same cut from two days ago
however much i scrub, bristles sprout from my body
with age bathroom tiles start resembling the color of humans
on the veranda sitting and smoking a cigarette, uncle
resembles a thick korean dictionary
the thin pages quickly turn over
the back door is erased, you have no place to visit

3

when i put my neck inside a t-shirt i think
last night thanks to dreaming of you
outside my heart a pouting signboard hangs
from the grime-worn floors rusty nail heads hammer
i bury you along with a set of chopsticks and spoon
tap tap tapping on a lukewarm tomb
the heels of dust, they rustle

K

the person who had been standing by the window is K. despite our eyes meeting, he seemed to have no intention of retreating from or fending off my gaze. outside the window the wind was blowing to and fro as if to fall on its back.

barely holding on to myself i thought i envied gray-haired K. because that time seemed so distant to me. past sunbeams burn up. what is burned up cannot come back into existence. let's say that is why i wanted to steal K's gray glimmering gaze. even if i had, i wouldn't be able to recollect that time, and even to imagine it is too difficult. it's like a window. a well-dusted, bright window frame.

that time. the textured crinkling of brown paper bags. the smell of cheap food that wafted from within. holding the paper bag. my eyes opening wide. the darkness thickening. at midnight when time almost smells burnt. that time when solicitors shroud the streets and the neon signs glow their brightest. i cannot know what K was thinking. this unhinges me.

K is dreaming and that is also my stance for thinking about K. to be standing outside all conceivable reactions. at the place of lightest weight that took me away. thousands of butterflies invented the person that is K. therefore. as ever. wings. the heat glowing from heaped wings. the place where K vanished. only a fever remains. blazes. that time. burnt-up K cannot stand in that place another time. wavering K is not K but is truly that K is

meanwhile

teardrops cry while the eyes cry nothing
the commotion occurred before i awoke
there is a shaking—a thing that is shaking
while the welling within me is something i pity,
after all pretending to be good or evil
is not something to be forgiven
a boundary bounds a boundary and
the act of counting numbers is not tedious
what will not end has been lost
it's best not to seek something like it
even forgotten, events in faraway countries are futile
power is heavy while names are near,
anyone thinks much too often
the world is the lumped form of thinking
living appears as is, hoodwinked
grayscale streets grow overcast
tragedy demands courage
i live in the house of conclusion

boy ivan

to ivan who woke up early this morning the kitchen was like a windless bamboo forest, silent—father, the face he left behind, when picked up, was cold as a dropped razor blade

the day was waning—ivan found an ear—late at night sitting on a secluded bench in the playground he tilted the ear to the sound of his own crying—was endlessly listening

every morning, ivan's cry-dangling ears heard a sound from the back of his younger sister headed to work—a sound as if something sparkly was sparkling

ivan shaved his face—mother became a spacious grove of silver grass, ivan became a swamp beneath her feet—except for this there's no way to describe mother's restless rustling

the more time passed, a dull, ordinary crying clung to the ear through unknowable effort—accordingly, ivan holds for his own ear a boundless pride

a certain chronicle

we recall a certain chronicle, and night pours above. one man soaks up the night while walking. from his back drifts the scent of timeworn paper. standing in front of a house, he twists and pulls the doorknob. he dusts off his shoulders and enters the house. that is all. without him, the street becomes empty. the traces of his footsteps fade into nonexistence. from time to time, the dead pass by. for a moment, all is quiet

in this chronicle there are traces of furniture. we briefly stand and then sit. because the snowy street is heavy, because most people become lightheaded when they behold something heavy

when it is time for the lights to turn on, one by one, the man's existence portrayed on the window draws out his stash of liquor. his hands have a habit of trembling. and so we must wait for him and this chronicle. as always, because sadness is like an unfinished house that wastes away, the man bears his flushed face as the damp gloom dribbles inside. the gloom will soon extinguish the candles, like a person who quivers from a single exhale. he cannot fall asleep, and we must tear out a page from this chronicle. for night always visits. for we have no right to leaf through his dreams

珉 [min]

to the girl standing next to me, unbeknown i give her a name i know—i didn't glimpse the face of the girl wearing the meticulous stockings, her bright fingertips peering out from long sleeves, neatly arranged—the sense of her brushing my shoulder each time the bus tilts, now and again, is it possible to love it so—outside the window, the unseasonable cold has drawn an impossible darkness—at this late hour where could she be returning from—the name i give her is 珉 [min]—no matter how hard i try, only a hazy afternoon comes to mind and i cannot recall the original owner of the name

your place

i am the person to your left, to your right—the person turning from left to right—if there is a person who sinks beneath your feet, i am that kind of person—i am the kind of name that disappears when you close your eyes—the falling rain disappears—i turn more and more into a large vanishing point—the corridor becomes a little colder—there you stand—what you had thought precious is an unknown face—there is a breathing sound with only the thorns remaining—only a single color remains—i loved that color—you are the person to my right, the person turning from right to left—if there is someone wobbling like a loose tooth above my head, that would truly be you—you are the person who completely erases me so

well of feelings

*

i threw myself into the water
the water might be our delusion
i might not have entered the water
water underwater flows as if weighed down
i might have been left behind again on the bare floor

*

i spoke like a stone
a secret must stay a secret
the sound of my words rolling
the sound of the water waking

*

i flowed underwater
at that time i had no face
without a face i also had no tears
our expressions might be our miscomprehension
drop by drop i might have drifted farther away

*

the waves splashing their mouths open
from far away they drew near
the sound that suffers sound
the sound of a person weathering weight

*

i sat underwater
stony like a ruptured rhythm
i moved nothing
nothing could move
nothing remained to flow

tomorrow and tomorrow

the two of us sit face to face, wordless like misdelivered lunch boxes, our fingers headed toward each other's eyebrows, foreheads, our shadows scattered into uncertainty, laid out side by side and drifting

we are separated by a raindrop—wanting to place my left hand on your right cheek, my feelings branching out—the window reflects our situation, the two of us sitting together—the sentiments of a lifetime, floating up and refusing to sink—for matters like this are like a loose, ill-fitting glove—i am in love and you are at a loss for words

i have never felt at home with this today that cannot be traveled further—with fingertips i stammer only what surrounds you—before i speak my lips are like a musical instrument i cannot play—for i wanted to place in your hands the quiet calm released to you, sitting across from me, to never return

an impossible distance says nothing until you look behind you until you look at what is behind from behind

the loose pages of time

at the full midday sun the walk had begun you would have led low-pitched steps up to that place one of the stooped leaves would have fallen in your direction your throat would have been parched like a song, you have gone astray while i cannot be certain since no one was there that place would not have been a place for you to visit the wind that drifts through july is cruel some things just float downstream to get here you would have cast off your good-natured will to uncover your gaunt arms like a face holding back tears two arms trembling while holding still, you would have left them trembling at that moment what was on your mind perhaps you thought about the deep night that can only be written down as a *desert* and its plight you were walking even when most of the streets disappeared without a trace i am sure of it people who cannot stand a single soul are like that people for whom there is nothing left to bury are like that it would have been better to not remember that night when the loose pages of time fly over and the strength leaves your fingertips the dog from the afternoon follows you and you pet the dog's head, holding onto the dog's scruff you would have walked along following the time pulled by the dog you may have even heard that at the bottom of the hill there is a blue ocean with what face do you look at the dog who looks back at you now and then no one instructs you on things like this you leaving your bare arms to burn in the sun you may have caught the scent of the ocean that may not appear and heard the waves in the distance and then briefly you may have gazed up at the sun the moment the world transforms into darkness there is nothing only you are there the faraway bark of the dog from the afternoon has everything been left behind i cannot be sure only that you followed down the hill and briefly pretended to look back you may have never returned after that although there was one dog who came back holding a single shoe in its mouth, if that dog was the dog from the afternoon or a dog with a darker coat even that i cannot know it is now just the time of conjecture and now people will discover one corner of their windows no one knows when the stain appeared but the bright and crimson smudge resembles a person so the people will whisper among themselves for quite a while the stories in those rumors someone will secretly record together with time

friday

the people dressed in black burst forth. pen clutched in hand, i am powerless. this divinity that transfixes time. the letters i trace with my darkening fingertips take flight. when the dark deepens and what we read as night glimmers. where did they go. and so, i no longer have faith in anyone.

dear most unhappy face over there, this place is filled with your failures. i become more and more cramped like a crumpled piece of paper. a long time has already passed since those who swarmed my desk have disappeared. so how weightless and solid is misfortune. now is the time for me to weep myself. when my hand touches my hand and my eye touches my eye, when my chest and back try to embrace—that moment.

discarded words

above the discarded words leaves break out and shake below the person who passes by after finding, blooming, placing, sometimes throwing, flowers as the wind blows as the blood strolls who searches the street with their back turned away endlessly to only suddenly wheel around above the discarded words friends visit there are people who watch askance there are people who rummage through diligently there are people who enter a narrow street corner and flicker their shadows in these moments the discarded words ache unnoticed and if there is a person who stubbornly dithers the distance between “no” and “yes” it is chilly like an office clerk who thumps their shoulders before returning to work there are things running down the hallway like a child with too many dreams imitating sounds, sinister sounds that stir up fond memories, so not totally useless, and wondering if they might be too old to pretend to not notice the sounds, the discarded words also sit on the terrace facing the throng

station

this place is a passage of worn out people. they usher their frayed legs up the stairs.

the train has not even once arrived on time. accordingly, clocks are as useless as the train schedules here.

those who departed early in the morning return past dusk. occasionally, those who arrive late into the night walk with an increasingly tattered gait.

the passage remembers one man's passing. his *causa mortis*: winter. when he was buried in the frozen earth, his wife wept with sorrow. like a train that was about to arrive.

memory is nothing but mere memory. similar to my hesitation to write when something comes to mind, the station does not move. no, the station sways a little each time a train departs. slowly at first, and then faster and faster, the station disappears.

23:24. yet another train will arrive from the city. the passengers preparing to disembark remain out of sight. no one is waiting to board.

the umbrella's hometown

outside the window a thinned, unnerving season
the young men, they walk past clutching language
i hadn't heard of birds that fly through the rain but
just now, something flew through the air

my tight fist turns white, i
am sitting in every empty space, i am also over there
faces where surprise slumbers, are swept away

it could have been a bird
the men turn back to pick up what was dropped
their corduroy pants are sad as they get soaked

that is how the umbrella is born, we
are born wet, are things living for wetness
like an answerless question

now is the time to visualize the umbrella's color
gently beginning, dark and familiar
the chill of the hand next to yours touching now and then

on a day like this when no tears are shed, everyone cries again
what flew away might have been the dusty dreams of birds
what becomes drenched might have been wholly rain

do you hear

do you hear, do you hear, my words.
the image my heart draws on my retinas,
when you said you would send hands to hold,
distant hands, i just laughed,
but then i began to believe, the darkness of my net-like eyes
are they dark, are they getting dark, my words?
now it is time to talk about the bright lights
when i took off my eyes and lay down, i learned
a light too bright brings with it an equally large
shadow to match. while i guess that's not all,
do you fear, are you afraid of, my words.
when distant hands arrive, you said to hold tightly
though you weren't going to visit, unblinking eyes,
once they quiver, leave behind a certain surrender,
again, i try to feel the slow touch of softness
mumbling that it won't be mine
do they cry, are they crying, my words.
two hands, covered by two hands set to arrive from afar
beyond the distance that grows and grows
do you see, do you see, my words.
not at all, not at all, i say, i don't think so and
i cry my words without knowing why.

peonies

the peonies you said you'd planted climb night and writhe into bloom, not knowing when these flowers are supposed to bloom and believing it is now summer, not knowing if you have a garden, and if not that, not knowing if you planted the peonies in a flowerpot or how the flowerpot glimmers brightly, not knowing anything, the peonies you planted arrive dragging the dark, from under my feet and up to my head, and again spreading into my nose and inside my breath, blooming from my mouth, why are such round things so bright, and if not that, how do i explain this moment never having been taught how, spring passes like this and it is summer again, i try sticking my body against the wall, and so, to call them peonies, i don't even know what those flowers look like, they are not me and even more so they are not you, the plant's name bobs in my mind like a ball, i am so very curious about the thing you said you'd planted and i wonder why i am so sick of such peonies, you who would have brushed off your hands loudly after planting them, those flowers, the peonies you said you'd planted, bloom and creep

trajectory

another person and i were sitting on a wooden bench. colossal clouds were crowding in. without any designs, slowly slowly dividing. yes, clouds. even in the distance, clouds. the two people sat on the wooden bench and watched the clouds.

the clouds slowly, still slowly. at a speed impossible to guess where they'll go. over there. they simply slid onward. the two people, they each said something, but nothing important. perhaps clouds are simply things you see. i was thinking only of someone else who wanted to *flop* onto a cloud, and so, again and again, *flop flop*, this sound went on and on

night arrived. the other person and i were no longer sitting on the wooden bench. we could only see a few clouds. and i liked that too. how the other person felt, i can no longer know.

erasable map

when night arrives i study my own ways to become a desert—to grow old even faster i walk slowly and walk backwards, turning around suddenly to remember someone i tried to forget, aching a little

a map is like an animal that grows in fragments—i consider my arid career of tearing open envelopes—although when i see the symbol called *father* i think about playing catch

and before you know it, twenty-thousand hectares or so of playing field grows between me and father—every now and then i secretly plant seeds the size of pill halves, but nothing grows

his back turned to the wind that just blew in, my sad and young self runs to pick up the ball—who are you, whose hide is this glove made of, and why do i start wanting to shout when i see an object in flight

the evening rings round and round with the cries from a little girl chasing her older brother—an evening where you hold your breath until you can't cry out another—perhaps the pattern of life is like that, like wrinkles on pursed lips

but the dead don't toss anything—the red sun crosses over to open the heart of a path overgrown into an unyielding hardness—it's been ages since i erased the way of sprinting to catch like this

neighbor

the tree branches in the empty lot darken into a thickness—it was that kind of summer

or maybe it was winter—such details are unimportant

with something akin to determination, i remember my neighbor standing under the blazing sun like a hardened piece of bread

he had moved in with just a single emaciated clothes hanger

the sun that day stooped down at a peculiar angle, and he was swaying a little, like a sloughed off overcoat

i pound on the iron doors of his house, sturdy as teeth, and ask, *who is it?* i am your next-door neighbor, could i perhaps borrow a candle? *there is nothing here* he has no further words for me through the doorknob—he stands in the dark and merely stares at the pale door

since the day he moved in i've grown thinner and thinner

on some early mornings, i hear an extended whistling from his house—i wake from my sleep, and with my neighbor's pet in mind, i curl up smaller and smaller into the awkward blankets—on those days, endless shadows fill my dreams, swaying little by little

he discarded the clothes hanger in a corner of the empty lot and moved away

i remember the sight of him leaving as something akin to a misunderstanding from time to time, i stand there like the wrapper freshly torn from a pack of cigarettes, and while hanging a shadow on the clothes hanger, i think—why is it that neighbors are such loose things, such dark and narrow hallways

like the shadow sagging on the clothes hanger, i sway slowly slowly

today's outside

a boy blunt as a pencil stub sat in the bookstore. the arm of the bookstore clerk on a ladder shone through her thin blouse like an endless bird wing

memory makes memory miserable. a person like the white fuzz that spreads along the edge of a skirt, the kind that multiplies the more you pick at it until scrapped

some moments resemble the sound of money being counted, piling up higher and higher. everyone has a hill like this. the sum of a day's work is memorizing each other's unpredictable heights and

while i open and read the sounds of cicadas heard at dawn i cry through the widened gap between my wings and back. when i cling to a person's side and squeeze in, and when i'm not there, i bustle about searching for my self

at night everyone lies down alone. to accomplish this familiar task i'm often laid out in a long thin line by morning. but there is no one who can guarantee this. for when finally everything goes dark

how cloudy is such a thing as *outside*? is there another word as easy to write as *today*? someone's scent, someone's touch, someone's lingering warmth, how many times do you turn inside out such absurd comedies again and again?

when you are here

and just like that, when i think you are here i shake and hang the laundry out to dry—i take a break from my cigarette and sit exactly as i am after inspecting all the nooks in the blanket—tilting my head to follow the sun that tilts all day, i listen for you and lift my heels in the direction of your arrival—lift up and bring down my arms slightly—when you, no, even when a shape resembling you approaches, i become a lousy reader who opens a book only to put it back down—in that moment i wonder how to place my hands how to laugh how to mourn in the loveliest way, and so you, you, your ways fold me, me away like wings—spilling, i look over my shoulder—your image suspends me in suspense, no, suspends me exactly as i am—if i could suspend and suspend suspension—recall, like a return among countless returning returns—if you could sit me down and sit by my side, lay me down and lie by my side—lie in wait and touch—a drawn loneliness pointing toward an empty spot in a world of nothingness—when i follow my hand and walk, it's as if i could simply pass through you, as if i could get to know you a little—the reason my breathing burns into a suffocating cinder that feels like stone and can only be felt as stone is not you but this pocket of reality—you, a maze always out of view, i stand behind your eyes and wait for you like i am standing by for an afternoon to be drowned in a deluge—i grit my teeth, grit until i pale with exhaustion—and somehow from yourself, at last, you arrive

the painter's room

shelved in the darkest corner of that bookcase, there is a book no one has ever read about an artist's life. the artist dedicated his entire life to painting a picture of a single room. the unfinished painting can be summed up as follows:

a person walking down a dark, cramped alley thinks about the interior of his room. if you could believe in something without question, that thing would be flames. inside, his hollow mother and hollow younger brothers and sisters and hollow shapes of people turning away and hollow shadows and hollow resentments, they all flicker. from somewhere, he hears a heavy sound, and the pitch-black time he believed would never arrive finds him. who measures the heft of our lives?

while walking over to the bookcase in the corner of my room to shelve a book, i stop to watch the fractured sunlight scatter in through the window. and the room the artist was unable to paint will swallow its own achromatic fear and stow itself away somewhere just a bit darker

PART II

father inside my coat

it is only after i lose my wallet that i find father inside my coat. he is holding a long and slender cigarette between his teeth. dear father inside my coat like wet feet, how do we make sense of this strangeness? i put my hands in my empty coat pockets and look back at father. birds fly up from the shadows. i am certain i saw them, the faint traces. father inside my coat is still cold, and i am at a loss. father. *yes?* are you happy? *why would i be happy?* then why did you do it? *that's a question i should be asking*. i raised my head in the direction that was disappearing. leaves swayed between the streetlights and the trees on the avenue. but it seems we must continue arguing, even inside the same coat.

today is

“today is a truly beautiful day,” so the saying said. i was at a loss for what to do. *well, there should be days like this, no?* no, it’s not that . . . *today the sky is truly blue.* the living room was dark.

whenever she was sick, she would recall shadows and sag with the wind. *what’s something that can’t cry when it’s young and only cries when it’s all grown up?* a frog? *no, a human.* humans do that? *that’s right, humans, that’s how they live.* that’s a lie. *you just don’t get it.* what don’t i get? *when you’re a little more grown up, you’ll understand.* you sound just like her, like mother lying in bed. a window eternally sick with shadows

pouring water into a cup, i was surprised to find myself crying. inside an even darker living room. *wait a minute, aren’t you me?* i asked. the water overflows in the cup, i cry, and i fall silent. like too much sunlight in a dusky living room. *can’t you stop crying?* i pitch the cup. what shatters is not the cup but all the water that can’t be contained. because i am sad, sadder, even a little more

and so, no wonder it’s dark. cold like too many replies, my body shivered. is someone there. they pass through the corridors echoing their hollowness. everything becomes warped. the saying no longer said anything. the day was already truly beautiful. i could hear the chatter of children. i could no longer see the sagging shadows. or that’s what i told myself can i stop crying, i ask only after i stop crying. it's always difficult to place hands on your own shoulders. it's disastrous to cry and then laugh. i said this while trying to place my hands on my shoulders. the shattered drops of water fill up the dark living room. i am commonplace, found anywhere, and so even crying alone isn't bad, this i stammer

just as it is, the living room is, the human being is, and i am, today is, today's truly beautiful weather is, the saying is, her illness and i are, someone's corridors are endlessly dark and damp, no, they are sorrowful and spilling

november 4th

it was an unusually dark night when the man borrowed the pen. he jotted something down onto the back of a large envelope in his hand. like yellowed street lamps late at night our eyes met a few times

where are you headed? he asked, returning the pen, *it's late no matter where you might be headed.* i didn't answer, and the people waiting for the last bus all gazed into the same spot, as if trying to hide their bodies, no, as if trying to get sucked in, like most nights

the man held out the envelope, *it's an address. i don't know where. it just occurred to me it might be something like a hometown i've never been to before.* i straightened my coat, you've never been there? *well, it could be that i've been there, but i can't recall*

i caught a whiff of something, but couldn't discern its origins. when the bus arrived at the station, only the man remained, like an unpocketed hand, having tossed night behind him, tilting his chin

and in that moment, i thought his face seemed familiar, but only in the way that countless things seem familiar. by the time the bus departed i had forgotten most of the episode, and only the place written on the back of the envelope came to mind. that place was a neighborhood full of narrow alleyways. the name of a place i've never been to before, that i no longer recall

a story only he knows

he sits on the sofa—the light is spent—outside the window it's getting dark—after a beat, the living room too

is getting dark—the second hand ticks—next door, a person lives—a wall stands—in a picture that hangs on the wall, snow heaps up—socks, dress shirts, teeth between a slightly parted mouth, they are bright—he is immobile, but ever so slightly, he moves—the words he spoke—the fingertips of his departed lover, the sound of their voice—when he recalls these things, in such moments

from the darkened sofa he sits—a heavy trace—beyond the window, always as if new, always in the same place—stars stud through from a departing cosmos—and perhaps he wants to cry, but perhaps it's just that the tears won't come out—perhaps, of his own accord, he's already becoming a single drop

snowfall

on streets blanketed in snow, the white-haired people walk warily. on this disquiet night, i grill pieces of gopchang and sit with the story of a young man's first love and the unsent letter he stayed up all night to write once upon a time. the man turns misty over the past, and above the butchered memories, the steam collects into a fog

believe it or not, while coughing, i think of the musical notes i clutch in my frozen hands. this bent present, all of it, is a song to me. the outside is, as always, what was swallowed and spat out by the winter of our youth.

how white it all still seems inside that time, the haggard name that is *us*. this night shrouded in snow resembles a vast cave. but to fall silent and face my burning face, suddenly, the next day, i ache with the fallen snow

how it goes

the men sing
they lick each other's names
and drink the backs of their hands
for all the things brimming
the door is far too small but
you can tell what it is

the men grow tipsy
under their gaze
a woman wearing makeup walks by
nothing is agreeable
this night just like that forgotten night

at home their wives
with what was forgotten
and with what was lost
will put the puzzle together
but that's how it goes

everyone is now a person who will fall asleep

the songs will end and after everyone leaves
the bar will lock its doors soundly
but in the end the end is unknowable

for now, no one has left
it's cloudy, and that's how it goes
a half of night, a night to get soaked in sleep

the whole of my hand

on a snowy day, in the swaying
car of the last train, my swaying hand
lay dying like a wet coat,
a thing too somber and thick
to move at all

spring then summer
back when the seasons were defined,
a time that exists for anyone
at least once
when everything is yours
back then
when each person caresses then clutches
like wind flowing into the sound of water
their own aloneness

gone, the warmth i wanted is no longer
mine, i had once written, in the
end, all pallid things are love to me
when my hand dies, all the names
my hand once held begin to wither
with an astonishing gloom
colossal and cold
they send their last greetings
the task of permitting a farewell
is the whole of my hand

falling inside

the time of the hairstreak butterfly flying away as a swallowtail butterfly, the time of sitting with my back turned, the time of the midday sun before its heat, the time of dust dividing and drifting away its numbers, the time of dandelion seeds floating up and sinking and floating again, the time of my aching eyes straining to see farther, the time of the houses stretching out faraway one by one until they disappear, the time that won't arrive, the time of snow slowly falling inside the soju bottle, the time of ressentiment, the time of trees locking up their shadows, the time of feeling enough time has passed while fearing that time will stop, the time that at any rate doesn't pass easily, the time of turning back again with a sigh, of snow falling still inside the soju bottle, of not yet being drunk, of my still aching eyes, of explaining away even the things too far away to see, the time that is you, the time that isn't you, the time that isn't me thinking of you, the time of discarding myself as such, the time that breaks, the time that melts, the time that blows away, the time that dissolves, the time of snow no longer falling inside the soju bottle, the time when there are no butterflies and only violets remain, the time of leaving behind the violets and returning, the time of no longer being there, the time when only time remains, when even time can barely stand to leave itself, that time

more beautiful than you

backs curl and curl as they are, as if to enter each other's bodies, licking each other's faces to write down their expressions

i hold a lost and sodden key to open a long-locked door as i step through i stand still to recall a time that is slowly fading the past savored in mourning is like the sound of crying daubed on a crumpled tissue

it always rained around me and i wished to become whatever the splendid surroundings asked of me on such nights the feeling of someone standing behind my back how anyone nurtures a back like a child

now, listening closely to such clumsy feelings, someone tries to close the door, the feelings melt away drop by drop, the moon's halo appears and the clouds gather

dialogue between two bodies stripped bare

he did not speak of that day.

of the sky that day, the blue day that turned violet, he did not speak of that day.

he placed his two hands on his knees. and this looked a little strange, like a book you stopped reading partway. when he closed his lips, i thought i had seen a flock of birds in flight.

and so, i did not speak of the dark, of the roaring sound and speed that pierces the dark, of the old snow that no longer melts. rather, i imagined how i wanted to open up and read the pages of his hands.

on reflection, i had never heard his voice before. we looked in different directions together as if we had declared silence—on impact and impulse, on language and gloom—while he did not say *it was people*, i think i heard him utter those words, and whether it was he or i who didn't say, that a wind had floated over to wrap me up and take me somewhere, i cannot know.

and just like that, we sat across from each other, whether we saw each other, or not. all i know is that i was the one straining my ears to listen at a loss.

the umbrella's course

on the topic of umbrellas i could talk at length—they are an inky light and i love the unfurled hours.

take the darkening streets, when people return home with their shoulders hidden, the streetlights turn on and the shadows disappear, when i stagger behind,

how to be born from inky waters or to live as wet bodies, how to lose or to forget oneself with ease, or perhaps how to walk alone

at the funeral i was the sole participant. while there was no forecast for rain, i carried a long umbrella and the sky shimmered in the hue of sorrow. the gravediggers all poured out a groan in unison. a staggering hole. but the dead won't return forever. i can't recall the color of that day.

what i lit again was an umbrella—it was a saturday and i walked calmly—the cars sped by in a frenzy and each puddle packed with bruises overflows, so what is there to do but retch

and so how can one not love the umbrella, whether long or short or folded up or unfurled, this existence that swells with memories

some newspapers broke the list of faces filled with holes—while everyone was appalled, the day passed without a single falling drop, as if nothing had happened that morning. the puddle i stepped on was long and narrow. i know someone with eyes like that. someone i met by chance. someone who held onto me and wept awhile. i can't remember why. i still don't know why the woman wept. slender, inky bobby pins trickled down from her hair, and yet, no one opens an umbrella.

well then, let's take a look, where do all directions go, is to be born to be dying why, is it that if you don't keep flowing you go mad

i stare at the weightless ceiling held aloft by enchantment and under the name pulled taut is where relief and contentment find their way to you

everyone gets flustered or lost while writing their own name, a name has never been sick—i want to love what's behind—the bones of love are long and narrow so,

there was a time when a priest dripping from the rain flickered by like a candle flame. he watched me from under an umbrella. i didn't mind if the scene was light. as if it amounted to something light and shiny like a coin to beg for, but a life might be like a packet of medicine you store in a drawer. because reality needs a place to be put away.

this is my long-held philosophy, i've talked about this topic at length, and while i'll talk for a while longer, if the topic is about a madman who gives names to umbrellas i do not confess to it and i do not hold it dear—even if it doesn't exist, i long for it and i do not live with it

and so, we must study the act of walking under an umbrella together, even if it serves a most bitter memory,

secret landscape

not a soul walks on these worn streets, and there, between the fallen shadows, i exist—clouds that will never return pass by—and because i didn't believe in crying, i wanted to cry like a child with a round candy in his mouth

as the dark lifts, everything sparkles—and what doesn't sparkle doesn't constitute everything—born into a slippery, light sleep and knowing nothing, i stretch out my cold hands—it sounds like someone is knocking on my door, and i look like i'm ready to close

or perhaps i'm standing on someone's gray coat—such a thing becomes a habit, a secret that everyone shares at this hour, and so, on trivial matters—recalling someone's pallid face or swallowing my own expressions—i don't take notes

standing there, what should i have borrowed—the memories that dry up and crumble without cause, they fly away and scatter—in any case, everything will continue to pass me by, i think, dusting the dark, and perhaps a thought like this is too coarse and transparent—yes,

this is what anyone wishes for themselves, i murmur—no, i'm not the one who murmurs—perhaps i'm the one who listens instead—from the brief shrug of my shoulders, i hear the sound of a door closing—now, even if i turn or duck my head, i won't be seen

and the children are dancing

the children are dancing
and under the gray ceiling
i can't fall asleep
the music plays on
until dawn arrives and
the dancing children since when
were you all there
i can't fall asleep
one is one and two is two
children are children
and i'm no longer invited
since when? since when!
one from two, from two to one
the children are dancing and the music plays on
i wish they would stop
but will the children collapse into tears
the dancing children won't cry
for too many people crying at once is scary and sad
on this night i give up on sleep while the children
dance and they don't cry so how
happy is it if i were to not fall asleep
after one, two, after two, three or two
and the children are dancing
and the children, they dance

again, erasable map

the bus doesn't arrive, the atmosphere is still—the clouds grow into the texture of water, and the humidity drags the sky with the force of a second

soon the music will begin to fall, the pleated skirts of school uniforms will sway above the live musical score—according to the weather report we are living in a season of rain—the bus stop has ossified, and the street lamps burst into a hard light

the blank sheets of young men close their shoulders, the rain comes into the world from hiding its body in the air—doesn't need a long way to go—even just five centimeters above your heart, rain will be born

caught in the newborn rain i consider how perhaps a map is inscribed into our steps, and how much i want a glimpse of this map

everything that bounds into the music is dear to me—the crying that sidestepped the rain watches me with large eyes—when the night of mother loving father and father searching everywhere for mother arrives

the forecasted, forgone moments bend their waists to see the contours—the whole map, everything that is pouring toward me, pours

handshake

—from the middle of certain travels

it feels like i've been carried along for a while *that's what traveling is like* it must have been quite some time since you departed . . . *excuse me, that sound just now, did someone pass by? shaking a set of keys*

silence then a sound as if someone is passing by, shaking a set of keys, dragging their steps

well, i only see shadows *i'm certain, there's someone over there* in that case, perhaps it's the ticket inspector . . . *my head hurts. please tell me about your travels* i don't have much to say about my travels. however,

silence then the sound of a shadow sinking into beams of light. as if someone is burning through

i do have this one bag, and when i come to my senses, i find myself neatly folded inside the bag, likely on my way to some destination until someone takes me out *is that the bag?* no, i've never seen the bag before since i'm always inside the bag *so you are inside the bag* . . . well, perhaps that isn't the case, or perhaps it is

a long silence then the sound of something getting dragged along like a heavy bag, the two people face each other

if we're talking about bags, i have a story for you. it's about a past lover. somehow long-ago loves remind me of bags, that is if you leave out all the shaking . . . perhaps you should stop the story there—some people have hanged themselves from that sentiment

a long moment, someone spits, but it's not them

the moonlight is rather peculiar, you can see the pine trees flocking toward the moonlight, and beyond, there will be an ocean because forests usually hide an ocean—look over there *oh my, it really is the ocean, the ocean in a place like this, what a relief . . .* you say it's a relief, how amusing

the sound of a train speeding ahead as if about to stop but with the will to never stop

i should probably get up are you getting off here *i'm not sure, i've been sitting here for so long . . .* you never know, perhaps you'll meet a certain someone carrying a bag *is that so* i suppose so

the sound of laughter, of two silent people, the two shake hands, their shadows grow longer, try to grow even longer without end

mister lee's worn boots

it's clear that those are not mister lee's boots. for whenever mister lee limped, the boots made a sound that didn't belong to him. the familiar sound reminded me of one particular man. he had wild eyes. he was the kind of man who'd spit whenever the wind blew on whatever wall was around. that sound, i don't recognize it, owing to what—a random fault or a sin i've committed—i don't know, all i know is i've dreamt about the worn and familiar sounds of his gait trailing behind me for some time now. mister lee climbs up the hill with a limp. because his steadily slowing gait is like a sad story passed on from memory to memory, because i will dream this again for a long time to come

the story of me and you

like the old Beatles song from the radio i recorded on cassette tape ten years ago, scratching, it's about to rain—because petals of wallpaper are about to fall, this morning makes my body ache—maybe the children cut loose the dog's leash again—i hear the sound of a dog running, a dog chasing down the alleyway, and the cheers of the children tailing after

lying side by side, knocking into each other, we live near the sound of the children calling the dog—between the dog's name and my name, the rain falls with outstretched claws, just enough so we won't look back

cold, i'm reflected behind this word and you are all the spittle spat out by sadness—one side sees and the other side forgets—i try opening my sight that is long gone and won't return—beyond my pupils, the bygone days that smell of antiseptic lie collapsed—the peculiar déjà vu where what lies ahead misses what is left behind and what is left behind endures what lies ahead—outside the window, your backs, like the sound of claws and

the same person

whether i close
or open my eyes
i see the same person
thousands, hundreds, tens
of just you
smiling slightly
i offer myself
to you to hold out
both hands on my face
both hands on my forehead
because it's always you
i close my eyes

the dark quiet

the wind dies—making such a strange racket—after the wind i've wound up pours, invisible hands stumble around and here i am—what other way is there to explain a person who has fallen asleep

a woman has dropped a photo—the woman dies—she leaves behind her body that ripples after death, look at that, it's like a comb with fine teeth—who knew this would be so painful

over there, to become indivisible, the water dies—and only after the water dies does it leave behind an undulating light—like finely combed dark hair or things likened to hair

outside the window the quiet flutters and is dead and gone—there's no way i'll go to such a place so far and too far to be seen—the past dies and disappears—the air is cold from the cries of an inconsolable child

what was dead has died—as can any season other seasons have left behind—the things i once held in my hands have died, the things that have died are trying to die, quietly, and just so

that winter

that winter—i wrapped up a long-term relationship and bought a blue safari jacket to wear until the season wore out—i can't remember the music i enjoyed listening to—i smoked a few packs of cigarettes and couldn't quit—i didn't shiver—it's just that nothing mattered that winter,

many people died—every now and then i looked at the electronic displays but didn't become the news—every now and then life was fine—every now and then a bird flew—every now and then i met someone i knew and exchanged business cards—wherever i went i carried my age like a backpack—my pancreas ached—i didn't take the medications prescribed for me—and just like that, another year was passing by—

the trees stood still—i wanted to write about winter but couldn't write—for everything seemed so useless, the letters i used to touch shivered in their bodies—many people lived on—old dogs climbed up the hills and the kids as always were good at running—

and that winter—the piece of paper i picked up was already crumpled—the things written on the paper quivered then poured out—it was all that winter—i hated someone with great care—he is no longer of this world—the only thing i could do was ask questions—i raised my hand straight up in the air and rose from my seat—but no one was there—

the winter always promised the next winter's visit—eternal farewells were either impossible or unknowable in depth—i was dying—salvation was everywhere but no one picked it up—i filled a diary with countless sentences, and i went on to erase even more—still, i couldn't quit—i didn't care about what could be so tough and persevering for no one peered into me—

in the end, are we deserving? i kept on hiding my hands, and while i was wary of my hands that kept on wanting to hide, my hands were completely guiltless—when my friends started to disappear one by one, i recollected their names and mused that we were now of that age—

there was something that was winding me up—i fell asleep often, and there were even nights when i could hear something snap—that year, i gave up on winter and at the same time wanted to see all the winters of that year—i was safe and that scared me—every time i thought this, i couldn't fall asleep—that winter, i blew in, blew away, floated away so far that i'm no longer in sight

PART III

the time that glimmers

after the promise, time
passes by fast and slow
again now everything
freezes into light

i am a part of my own beast
i will step on this shadow to rise
and amount to nothing
i will erase my breath and blood

my flesh, my bone, the woman, the dog
the line of lines that pierces through all
the bruised skies that surround me
from the first day until now
everything will be ruined

and so, let this moment be nothing more
than the edge of a knife

words left to say

the youths who live with slit wrists
grow thinner, unable to eat
caress their bodies of bones
to make music

i bring up a person to consider how
moments of memory, unfurling
into my past, could perhaps
be born again

i hoped you would wipe my eyes
until my tears sparkled
stop being you, please
i'll become you but
i've always been unlucky

the scars that hurt not knowing they hurt
the expressions i don't recognize as my own
hang on with no intention of letting go
while i had words left to say
my want for the next life was

unbearable feelings
that's how people learn to speak
even if i die the day after tomorrow
i won't say i'm sorry

scene

i am blue lips, a cold scent
a scene held by a gaze
that walks around picking up years

there is an age in our life
that runs faster than a ball thrown by the boys
and the memory of another age
that runs away screaming like the girls

how is it that over there
an empty lot came to be
and this version of me
takes after my parents and is dying

is marching on, crying as the crying
illusions of this world
the white bones of my blood grow limpid
drip-dripping away to melt and snap

now when the sun is supposed to set
everyone turns their clocks back
it's much colder than you expected
shivering as if to collapse

as if to burst into laughter
a breeze with a short shadow blows by
like a missewn doll
like a child chewing on a doll

there's a danger that grows more dangerous
and so, to be remembered as a denouement
an end no one has ever seen, the future arrives

boy

the boy was crying
with a sound never heard before
teardrops were falling

the teardrops well and welled into a bird
the bird looked long to one side
then flew in the direction of its gaze

the air, swayed then rippled
with water that had never fallen before
began flowing

and just as the moon was rising
the boy briefly forgot how to cry
listened to the reflection of the moon

the water walked into the water
deeper and deeper with faraway eyes
did nothing but run clear and fish-damp

what began to spread, to draw out tears
searching through a time that has never arrived
the silvery shaking that must be silvery

the wind trembled then blew like a trace
the moon the bird and that place melted
sizzled into a pour of scarlet rain

the boy who had stopped crying, when he touched the rain
each drip and drop became a cloud
the boy stood in the water for a long long time

unhappy reaction

1

like a melody stitched to your lips, some things are dreadfully hard to forget
like back then, a faded face in a time that wasn't
my body swayed, slightly
only after the person had disappeared
between the dazzling light filling out the borders of their sunken face

2

i heard the unhappy news
a crying person always turns in the same direction
i don't believe in my lot in life
the present always moves like teardrops

3

the voice that wells up in my throat, the paper-white letters that can't be written, the music that covers my ears, that becomes today and then suddenly stops
today is unbelievable

4

crying, i spoke—the crying cut off my words and my words mixed with the crying turned into an unintelligible sound that tugged at me, always countless, you and you all

5

black keys press my fingers
stripped tones tug at my ears
my hearing overflows
my pain suffers through me
burrowed memories that won't emerge
how do you endure something like this
i won't agree to my shame

untouching story

oh, the moon was out, but i only noticed the glow after its wane—i stood for a long time with my ear to the night—it was one of those faraway nights like someone could touch the sky to paint the back of their hand pitch-dark

the place once lit, then left behind, i call *flower*—the many things i wanted to show you, the many things shaken off the bough by a passerby, i decided to call these *shadow*, and so—all flowers must be shadows

as i let go of the words that were, my eyes closed slowly, i wanted to close them—that didn't mean i wanted to let go of your wrists, but in a slow slipping away i closed my eyes

calling even this a *wish*, the wobbly wind blew into an airy desire—no matter how much i tried to hold on, there was only air against empty air—traces bloomed in each of the places i cried out—i didn't touch those places—and even let go of the strength to break off a shadowy bough

the umbrella's antonym

i wish to become a puddle
in the heart of this sleeping city
there is doubt, a trace
we cannot seek

a glorious sound like this
is from a thousand years ago
forgive all the teeth
the rain tears apart tomorrow
pitter-patters eyelashes
to let out letters

words pour from my mouth
speechless eyes and water welling

a person whose mouth
is shut for as long as it rains
even if this isn't the case
in the face of weather like this
everyone is too open and transparent

refusing silence, they rise up
the words i want to say, i erase them
soaking from the outside in

B

why did B die leaving behind his belly, why did i hold dear b's body part that had looked so different from before, B who had to leave his home tongue to trace the letters of a foreign language

every street overflows with fallen things, B is a breeze about to get a little colder, b is the back of a sycamore leaf, B is the boxer briefs my little nephew left behind, what do you mean a life without a base, what you hit with your left palm is your own right cheek, B is yesterday's bearings, v is b's misprint, B is your name unknown even to you, my grandfather who tried to draw his last breath in secret stopped trying to pronounce b and instead lifted his thumb into b (the incident saunters by sliding along the right-hand walls of habit and the back-bent shadows lengthen and disappear and reappear and if you're surprised by this, then you have been abandoning jobless B)

yesterday a lie with a mischievous heart artfully ducked and lifted its head and tremble-trembling as if nothing had happened tried to leap into a perfect universe and then stopped as B, B who yesterday forgot today and today is trying his best to remember today—because meaning bumbles and is bumbling, the bare relief of language hollowed to the bone

the goat's forest

—J, what makes us walk on air

i once saw a goat. it ate white paper and grew a magnificent beard. with each bleat, a single basket appeared. i began to like the goat.

the trees in the forest bear mushrooms in secret. when you pick and eat the mushrooms—the goat tells me—you get to learn the fog, the dark, the weeping, you get to know the vomiting, the diarrhea, the fever.

however, the path to the forest is blocked. and the only thing able to pick the mushrooms is the goat. with its brilliant beard hitched up in a haughty expression. and because i like the goat, the goat can do as it pleases.

that night, i untied the leash around the goat's neck. the goat headed straight for the forest and never returned. and the goat's owner was unable to enter the forest.

unsent letter

K hyung, i am thinking of you. you are probably caressing an empty glass right now. until someone fills that glass for you, i've made up my mind to think of you

it is desolate here. because there's no one here to recognize me. to tell you the truth, i wanted to be alone. like walking while stepping on the soles of my feet, like when i gaze back and still find myself. there's no field here either. it's always been like that for us. i'm thinking how even this place would be a bit better if you were here, hyung. i guess it's the same no matter where you are. it's spring here too and dust-like particles are flying around. while i guess such things are fond memories, as you know, there is nothing left for us, nothing for us to leave behind. it all just seems like dust

i don't think i'll be able to finish writing this letter. i've known all along just like you've known me all this time. so K hyung, what more could i possibly say. our time was so short and even if that entangled time were to visit me again, i've made up my mind not to search through my pockets for you. hadn't we cherished the time we spent so completely absorbed?

when i think about how far away this place is, i find myself resenting you. that is, much more than what i expected. in all the alleys, i can see your eyes *how-your-large-pupils-storm-and-fly-through-the-air-from-below-from-above-flitting-they-stop-on-the-side-of-the-road-and-then-when-i-notice-i-cannot-stop-breathing-at-that-speed* and every time i gaze into your eyes, it's agony, something the likes of you wouldn't dare understand

K hyung, you already know this. that, there's no one who can fill the smooth emptiness of your glass, and so, hyung, you'll always thirst but,

it's okay to leap through the depths of time and it's okay to not. it's fine if we know and fine if we don't, i give you permission to do what you want. in this place, i'm trying to bear this bad and unusable story. and who knows, if i will be able to remember you fondly, or perhaps if you, hyung, will be able to remember me fondly, if something like that would be possible

thirty

in this time, this now, that is so obvious as to be unobvious, antlers sprout and fill with dozens of holes, and because i can't fill these holes, i love

this love has no teeth, no tongue, no arms, and even with nothing, these shitty tears shimmer for holding onto regrets is regretful

i keep having dreams about dying, dreams in which i, or my other self, die, the kind of dream that crumbles without leaving anything behind, where only verbs remain in operation, and i am unable to breathe

this name, a name i've stretched into oblivion, i marvel at this baggy name i no longer recognize

and so, right about now, i am a creature with only its antlers remaining, the creature of *us* and its cage, what i mean is, the creature we keep at the same time, if such things existed, would i be happy to live in that time?

wanting to linger like a smell that only lives behind walls, i would be happy to live just that much, truly, would be content.

empty frame

he takes down the snow-covered
roofs and the poor trees
a sorrowful picture

the picture is his
he hung it himself
over his shoulder his steadfast heart
at last flutters like dust

in the kitchen by the living room
a woman has broken a bowl
the raw flesh of crockery
laid bare like a scold

the exposed wall is bright
how did it happen
that the days that were, are sadder
than the days that won't be

nothing radish

i had left the house to buy a white nothing radish when snow began to fall like nothing with the greens chopped off—you, what nothing did you imagine for the falling snow to be this white, and so, i walk through the white snow—a young man falls, gets back up, and dusts off the snow, his coat is cloudy, the snow falls again fumbling for a familiar image—i look up into the silence—tomorrow i will lay out the pieces of nothing to dry—such crunchy conditions i find funny and thus sad—the things that will be swallowed up together and even the things that are becoming lost to memory

people from the past

on a winter's night i've eaten noodles in broth. snow is imminent. people from the past pass by. i know them. one child as ever refuses to take off his thick glasses. i'm afraid of the people passing by from the past. one man grabs and shakes my icy hands. his eyes wide open. frozen, my face refuses to leave his gaze. while a frightful chill fills the depths of my body, they drag away the things i know. the darkness falls. the snow falls in jagged intervals. the people from the past, their shadows are crowded with holes. they appear from behind like the dark. they are, now, unseen.

time being aloft

1

this is a poem about moored time
slightly feverish, when you cleared the window with a tissue
the seasons were all starting too quickly
the broad-shouldered men left the city
to put together the sky—soon, what they dropped,
the pieces of sky, will shake the ground
the clock in the living room stops and i lie in bed
thinking about a family history harassed by a shabby illness
we who have fallen asleep like pests to kill

2

on occasion, i have an amblyopic dream
the voice of my dead father, makes my heart grow
a landscape of sound without a soul around, suddenly
the timeworn path drops its arms in defeat
slowly cuts its breathing and i am a person
whose memory is worse than his appetite
the name i had created for a son is already
lost to memory, so father
please don't talk to me

3

my son with dark eyes
enters the courtyard of an ancient palace to gather
light—o, the sun is always full
however, because i prefer the shadows
with a stubbornness that hasn't seen a single kidney bean sprout
i nurture shadows without end—they say the nameless trees
become a forest right before they die and so
trees make for cruel burial sites—i
wished for you to be born as an instrument made of wood
your sire a musical score of no renown
your mother a listener of music
your aunt a child who cried at the smallest sadness
and so, my son, shoulders aren't something you take after
but something you take, remember this—the world
and the kind of determination it takes to be born

4

the children who have lost the ball love the ball
and we remember them and everyone is bound
to have at least one vacant lot they've lost—a wolfish moment
explodes—and laughing, chasing after the ball the disappearing
children—there are no shoulders that suit me—these bones, an old
inheritance—the skeletal remains of the distant future turn to dust
and pour—shake out the empty body and scrape together a tomorrow
i cast a shadow like a dark paper bag

a soft shade

a quiet book is laid out, i get in a taxi, go far away—i close the door that opens again—you are still unknown—the sound you dropped like a cup—i never imagined a corner could be so dark—i inscribe a few words—the book's cover is quiet again

i get out of the taxi, close the door and consider how many doors i've already closed today—behind the door is another door and behind that door you remain in the dark

and you will remain there for longer—the sharp sound pricks my fingertips and darkness is always anywhere—even here, the shadow sitting above the words is the final page of this silent book—i study and love the bright blank sheets of paper—so that they can't drift over—at last, this much, endless

back then

back then we were kids with our hands in our pockets—we walked slowly up the hill—when we looked back, the shadows grew longer—back then, what did we picture—one of us spat, a broken mirror blazed up, but each shard was as cold as shattered ice

one of us picked up a piece and threw it, aiming at the sky above us—our eyes stung—one of us wimpered, i don't think it was me—*don't sing along—don't clap along either*—we swore this—did we—probably, perhaps—the sun that once unfurled the wind had already long sunk—we are kids who haven't removed their hands from their pockets—who held my hand back then, one of us

we loved the dark that wound around us we bowed our heads toward the light—i can finally say it—the one of us was actually me—because the shadows that have already gone have grown so long—because we didn't sing together, back then

clear day

the word *jjamppong*, no matter how you say it, never grows sad
like a taut figure-eight knot that won't become undone, a hangover
is hilarious, in the way of most bad habits
like when water tastes of jjamppong broth, maybe
from the sky that suspends a bird, a plane, some unidentifiable object
something will begin to fall—on a day like this i want to see
the wife i don't have sitting at the kitchen table crying big fat tears
and in front of her, pulling up an ashtray, cigarette between my teeth
feel like the monosyllabic husband who studies his wife
and it's clear there's no way to know what that truly feels like
no matter how much i search this heart that won't play nice
it's only full of letters that won't be tamed
the word *jjamppong* is a little sad and too funny, so when
daily life bubbles and boils up like today's morning
i'm handed books delivered in bulk, how precious
there i am, signing the three characters of my name carefully
there i am, writing down the same letters again and again trying
to wring out my giddily laughing tongue into an apology

fragments of my youth

the schoolbag is falling
i pick up a piece of white chalk
and if not chalk, at least a nail
i bound down two steps at a time
the corridor rings with a taut tinniness
the corridor walls are cold
the sound of someone opening and shutting a mailbox
the schoolbag is falling
i am making a sound, crying
i go down into the dark basement
brimming with the odor of collected dust
i spit out and take another breath
the weightless window pane shatters
from my hand from my arm blood drips
bloodstains, they crust over, can't be removed
i bound up two steps at a time
the sound of labored breathing
i am a step short
the schoolbag is falling
i am crying out loud, no my mother is
a hilltop drenched in the afternoon light
a baseball hidden by a forest of gingko trees
the schoolbag is falling
i carve my name in secret and
slam, the sound of a window shutting
from the fifth floor to the first
the sound of my crying opens its mouth wide

the sun that hasn't finished its homework leans over
the shadows that spin around their bodies
mothers, a summer when they sit in a row
fathers, bringing home senbei crackers
on a day smaller and more solid than the palm of one's hand
the schoolbag is falling
the schoolbag is still falling
there's no way the schoolbag will ever fall
before the schoolbag, its shadow crashes first
the sky that pictures someone's face
the paints becoming a painting
even though the schoolbag is falling
even though night is still falling, with an iron will
still crying, i am hungry, *umma,*
umma, i cry out and go home
there's no way to fetch a schoolbag that hasn't fallen
a night when the security office is dark, i turn on the lights
the young hours are unable to fall asleep
my young self is still counting numbers

myeonmok-dong, seoul

the wife was tipsy from a half bottle of soju—the husband heaved his wife who would be sick all the way home onto his back and stepping out the front gate looked behind him—the docile quiet of the world laid out without incident

the husband couldn't know why his wife had wept—perhaps he would never know—not that knowing would make a difference—the husband, gathering up his slipping wife, became an empty bottle

the wife, secretly awake, was trying to bear her own weight—*i don't know if this warmth is my husband's or the night's—will there be another night as dark as this*—as she blinked her eyes she was drawn asleep

the stars were awake in the sky—the june wind breathed—the time that had passed became clouds and flowed—the street lights flickered and someone was singing—except for these two, the only other things on the street moved ever so slightly, a dog barked

back then, this was all me—the only ones who didn't know i was there were the husband and wife—blood began to stir in my heart—this is how the story began

Untimely Memorials: Attending to the Translation of *Today's Morning Vocabulary*

When I put my neck inside these poems of Yoo Heekyung, I think—today is a fine day for mourning, but with what language?

A vocabulary. A dictionary. A collection of words, names, appellations. When you recall a person, a memory, or a feeling, what words do you use?

The first time I read the book's title in Korean—오늘 아침 단어—I immediately heard it inside my head as *Today's Morning Vocabulary*. Though the serendipitous homophone of *morning/mourning* doesn't exist in the Korean, the pairing is fitting as the poems in Yoo's debut collection are fulgent and funereal, as tender as an aubade.

I frequently introduce Yoo Heekyung as a contemporary South Korean poet, playwright, and essayist who runs wit n cynical, my favorite poetry bookshop and project space in the world. Through his work, Yoo has made a name for himself as a cultural programmer and producer of a wide variety of poetry events and happenings throughout Seoul.

Born in 1980, Yoo is the author of more than ten collections of poetry and prose and his writing has been published widely in anthologies, journals, and newspapers across genres. Yoo studied creative writing at the Seoul Institute of the Arts (SIA) and playwriting at the Korea National University of Arts (K-Arts). He first debuted as a playwright in 2007 through the Seoul Theater Association's New Plays Festival before debuting as a poet the following year in 2008, when his poem "when i put my neck inside a t-shirt i think" (the second poem in *Today's Morning Vocabulary*) won the spring literary contest sponsored by *Chosun Ilbo*, a major South Korean daily newspaper. He is a playwright with the experimental theater company *dock* and a member of the poetry collective *jaknan*. Since his debut, Yoo has been awarded major literary awards, including the Hyundae Munhak Literary Award (2020), which aims to recognize the most outstanding works of Korean poetry, fiction, and literary criticism each year, and the Gosan New Writer Award (2019).

I first became aware of Yoo Heekyung in fall 2019 through a literary translation workshop during my final year in the Literary Arts MFA program at Brown University. Sawako Nakayasu, who was leading the workshop, connected me with the poet and translator Don Mee Choi for recommendations of South Korean poets I could translate. Don Mee recommended Yoo Heekyung. Yoo had studied with the poet Kim Hyesoon at the Seoul Institute of the Arts, and, in addition to his poetry, wrote plays and ran a poetry bookshop.

While pondering whether to translate Yoo's work, I read, watched, and listened to conversations and interviews about his motivations for opening a poetry bookshop. I learned that prior to opening the store, Yoo had worked as a literary editor for around a decade, when a retinal detachment caused the loss of vision in his left eye. Bedridden for weeks and faced with having to relearn how to read manuscripts with only his right eye, Yoo decided to pursue a long-held dream to create a space dedicated to poetry. With the support of his family, peers, mentors, and community, he quit working as a full-time editor and opened wit n cynical. In 2026, the bookshop will celebrate its 10th anniversary.

In an interview recorded shortly after wit n cynical opened its original location near Sinchon Station, Yoo can be seen sitting behind a desk in a t-shirt, providing a matter-of-fact answer to why poetry is important. His answer showed me who a poet could be as a person and a profession. He spoke about finding ways of helping a wider audience experience poetry in their everyday lives. Poetry both as art and air, something that anyone could cultivate a taste for as long as they could attend to what they liked and enjoyed. I was deeply moved by Yoo's efforts to create a more approachable, everyday culture of poetry.

I ultimately chose to translate Yoo's first poetry collection, *Oneul achim daneo* (오늘 아침 단어), because the translated title spoke to me. It felt important to my work as a diasporic poet who grew up learning and relating to language as a site of mourning. After learning about Yoo's work as a poet in the wider Korean literary scene, I wanted to translate his first poetry collection to be in conversation with his early work as an emerging poet.

I sensed a deep personal connection between Yoo's exploration of daily sorrows and my own experiences with both languages of mourning: Korean and English. I grew up speaking Korean with my family and within a large Korean enclave in the metro-Atlanta area, but I don't often use Korean outside of my immediate family. Speaking Korean has had a circumscribed existence for me. And as I grew up learning English in school, I was often asked to serve as a translator and interpreter for my family between the two languages, a task that could be taxing, though necessary and common.

So, for most of my life, learning and working in Korean and English has never been truly by choice. In college, I took Korean language electives because I feared that I would lose touch with my family if

I didn't continue with Korean coursework. Maintaining my Korean was less about expanding what was possible and more about managing the inevitable loss and lonesomeness when, at some point, I would no longer have anyone left to speak Korean with.

In another interview, Yoo shared that he hoped to remind people that everyone is alone in the world, and how that's okay because we're all alone together. According to Yoo, if you read a book of poems and come away remembering one or two lines, or finding a line that you like, that's enough. I found his inviting attitude towards poetry to be refreshing and liberating.

During this time, I also learned that Yoo wrote most of the poems for his debut collection in the aftermath of his father's fatal car accident when Yoo was a college student. In some articles, Yoo describes this experience as one of growing up overnight from a boy to becoming the head of the household. While *Today's Morning Vocabulary* is dedicated to his mother, a significant portion of the collection deals with the loss and absence of his father.

> to ivan who woke up early this morning the
> kitchen was like a windless bamboo forest, silent—
> father, the face he left behind, when picked up, was
> cold as a dropped razor blade

In "boy ivan" we meet a youthful speaker who encounters the strange, quiet domestic morning of the kitchen—when he picks up a photo of his father, or perhaps, recalls his face, his father's absence feels cold and cutting. At the playground, the boy picks up an "endlessly listening" magical ear that allows him to not only hear his own crying but to hear the quiet grief of his sister and restless anguish of his mother.

> the more time passed, a dull, ordinary crying
> clung to the ear through unknowable effort—
> accordingly, ivan holds for his own ear a boundless
> pride

In this story, or "poem-riddle" as critic Youna Kwak sometimes describes Yoo's poems from the collection, ivan's ear has been forever touched and sensitized to listen for loss and sadness. Rather than being a misfortune, though, perhaps it is the ear's inordinate ability to feel and hold sadness that makes our ivan a lucky fool.

Today's Morning Vocabulary was first published in June 2011 as the 393rd volume in the contemporary poetry series from Moonji Books. One of South Korea's most storied literary presses, Moonji is operated by and for writers and critics. It is especially renowned for its poetry series and its dedication to publishing literary works.

In the official press release written by Lee Kuenhye, the editor-in-chief of Moonji Books, the publication announced the arrival of a quiet yet bright voice on the vanguard of South Korean poetry, notable as the first in the Moonji poetry series by a poet born in the 1980s—a poet whose work represented a departure from the critically delineated Miraepa poets of the early 2000s, who in the aftermath of the IMF crisis rioted against the Korean poetic tradition through their vibrant wordplay, provocative imagery, and discordant anti-lyricism. Articles at the time of the book's release place Yoo within the Post-Miraepa, or those poets who carried on the avant-garde Miraepa sensibilities while embracing a return to the lyrical.

In the critical essay that accompanies Yoo's debut collection, literary critic Cho Yeonjung witnesses in these poems "the happy return of the unhappy lyric".[1] Cho's incisive and generous essay provided me with an opening into Yoo's rainy yet iridescent, overcast yet playful world. Cho notes in Yoo's poetry a sensibility more resonant with South Korean poetry from the 1990s, and reads in Yoo's work influences from Lee Seong-bok and Ki Hyungdo. I interpreted this to mean that Yoo's debut poetry collection eschewed a provocative edginess in favor of a phenomenological revolt of the quiet and quotidian.

While melancholic, his poems reintroduce readers to poetry that makes us feel and sense ourselves and the world anew. In the damp, at times cold, pages of *Today's Morning Vocabulary*, Yoo presents lyrical lineated verse and prose poems that chronicle contemporary life in a minor key unconventional for its mundanity.

On a lighter note, in "clear day," the speaker finds wry humor in his hangover habit while contemplating the funny-sounding *jjamppong*, a Korean hangover food classic featuring thick noodles and seafood suspended in a spicy broth:

> the word *jjamppong*, no matter how you say it,
>   never grows sad
> like a taut figure-eight knot that won't become
>   undone, a hangover
> is hilarious, in the way of most bad habits

1. This translated concept appears as "불행한 서정의 행복한 귀환" ["Bulhaenghan seojeongui haengbokan gwihwan"] in Cho's critical essay titled 「최초의 감정」 ["Choechoui gamjeong"], which in translation refers to first, beginning, and emergent feelings. Cho's essay is published as a commentary in Yoo's debut collection.

While the "sky that suspends a bird, a plane, some unidentifiable object" holds uncertainty for the speaker, in a sad and funny mood, he scries from a hangover cure a cliched domestic kitchen table scene with a crying wife and a "monosyllabic husband who studies his wife" while holding a cigarette between his teeth.

In "snowfall," I can imagine a scene with a young man catching up with an older colleague or mentor over gopchang, a popular offal-based dish often paired with soju on a winter night. His mentor recollects and shares a story of unrequited love from his own youth as they grill and consume the insides of another animal:

> on streets blanketed in snow, the white-haired people walk warily. on this disquiet night, i grill pieces of gopchang and sit with the story of a young man's first love and the unsent letter he stayed up all night to write once upon a time. the man turns misty over the past, and above the butchered memories, the steam collects into a fog

The speaker, reflecting on "what was swallowed and spat out by the winter of our youth," aches remembering perhaps a recent romantic loss or the coldness of holding onto what might feel like the last days of youth.

Loneliness, loss, and existential ghosts wandering the purgatory of youth—in this case, perhaps the forever adolescence of feeling brought on by life events—thread the pieces. The death of a parent. The strangeness of others. The strangeness of oneself. Reflecting on your own mortality. The minute and major griefs of daily living. Unrequited love, or the burn of waiting for the arrival of someone who is becoming beloved to you.

"when you are here" is one of the collection's many exceptional poems that capture the bittersweet feelings in romantic love that render the speaker devastated with both desire and the anticipation of loss:

> in that moment i wonder how to place my hands
> how to laugh how to mourn in the loveliest way,
> and so you, you, your ways fold me, me away like
> wings—spilling, i look over my shoulder—your
> image suspends me in suspense, no, suspends me
> exactly as i am—if i could suspend and suspend
> suspension—recall, like a return among countless
> returning returns—

Waiting for the object of his desire is agony for the speaker, and yet the poem stays with these overwhelming feelings that fold in on themselves. These are poems that bear witness to the quotidian feelings and phenomenology surrounding life-changing events. Or as critic Youna Kwak sees in Yoo's poetry, "Yoo Heekyung creates situations in which a speaker flails against phenomenological limits that curtail his attempts to fully apprehend the world," and reflect a "concern with how to recognize, describe, and account for our relation to others . . ."

In Yoo's poems, we see the emerging subject learning to hold their own manifold sadnesses. And yet, Cho notes that Yoo's collection resists providing readers with a feeling of easy or "expert sympathy." These poems create a small lit corner for readers to feel and mourn daily sorrows with compassion and resolve, as novitiates to life's emergent feelings.

In "in dreams," the opening poem of the collection, the speaker, suspended in a hypnagogic dream world, creates a light from beholding themself—whereby providing comfort for one's deep grief, the self can sublimate its own crying by tending to it.

> i held my being softly
> i beheld my cradled self
> a bright light glowed
> the rest remained in darkness

Similar to the speaker of this poem, as readers we prepare to attend to our feelings and the feelings we will encounter in *Today's Morning Vocabulary* and life events in all their light and shadows.

In translating Yoo's work, I find that his poems often provide the reader with both the rain and the umbrella. This is a world where even sadness has its own silvery sparkle. That is, feelings can change—by paying attention to them, noticing them, sadness and grief can transform and sublimate into something else, become a kind of anticipation, excitement, longing: a fluttering.

In "secret landscape," the speaker who haunts empty streets suggests that the conditions of light outside change how an object appears, and as time passes, the feelings we remember or revisit through memory or a poem might appear with different contours.

> as the dark lifts, everything sparkles—and what doesn't sparkle doesn't constitute everything—born into a slippery, light sleep and knowing nothing, i stretch out my cold hands—it sounds like someone is knocking on my door, and i look like i'm ready to close

These poems give readers permission to excavate and sift through their own losses and loves. To explore hidden monochromatic landscapes within memory, "dusting the dark."

When you stroll through the tripartite streets of poems in this collection, you walk backwards in time, or through memory in reverse chronological order.

In one of our email exchanges, Yoo referred to the chronology of the three sections in *Today's Morning Vocabulary* as a Proustian gesture, where the sadness of the present (that is, the sorrow of existence) reveals its origins as you move back through memory and story. The poems in part 1 largely deal with the present of the speaker; part 2 with the recent past; and part 3 evokes a distant past. Instead of Proust's madeleine, here we might find Yoo's t-shirt, umbrella, sycamore leaf, a dictionary, an old tape recording that sounds like the scratching of rain against the window, a piece of hardened bread. These each point to an origin story of the poet and his poetics.

This collection, as in some debut collections, serves as a bildungsroman tracing the origins of a poet's poetics and making. *Today's Morning Vocabulary* is a declaration of a poetics of loss, mourning, and renewal through the creative act of remembrance. The collection traces one emerging poet's affective biography as he becomes a poet by attending to the feelings of everyday moments with life-altering potential.

The poems in *Today's Morning Vocabulary* wear their feelings like a heavy overcoat. They are sentimental in the best, most consistent way possible. They are pathetic, in the sense of Eileen Myles' pathetic literature. They also recall for me Kafka's axe that breaks open the frozen seas within us.

Yoo's literary career includes extensive writing for performance as a playwright. Some of his pieces, such as "trajectory" and "handshake," read like short plays or descriptions of scenes. His poetic language often gestures at monologue, soliloquy, and dialogue to imbue his poetry with a level of conversational and emotional intimacy. His linguistic experiments play with the ever-evolving tension and slack between the reader and the speaker of the poem. Yoo sees poems as a chronicle of a person's thoughts and one of the few ways to interface between the self and other.

Today's Morning Vocabulary ends with the beginning and echoes the image of the speaker in utero. In "myeonmok-dong, seoul" the narrator, the poet, not yet a glimmer of a word, quietly observes the world as the husband carries his sleeping wife on his back: "the stars were awake in the sky—the june wind breathed—the time that had passed became clouds and flowed—the street lights flickered and someone was singing . . . blood began to stir in my heart—this is how the story began."

Yoo is unassuming when asked about the impact of his debut collection and the influence he and his generation of poets have had on the South Korean literary landscape. He mentions that his generation has made poetry more accessible to the public and helped to popularize poetry by bringing it into the everyday through a more conversational tone and language. The original Korean version of *Today's Morning Vocabulary* has sold over 17,000 copies, and my translation is based on the 14th printing from 2019. I mention this detail as Yoo routinely makes edits between printings—a reminder that revision is forever.

I sometimes imagine Yoo as a time-traveler, as a contemporary in the way Giorgio Agamben describes contemporariness through Roland

Barthes's summary of Nietzsche—"The contemporary is the untimely." More than one person has described Yoo as having the demeanor of a seonbi, or the poet-scholars of the Joseon dynasty (1392–1897) who served the public by sharing their knowledge. The poet Oh Eun, Yoo's close friend and fellow member of *jaknan*, who debuted before Yoo, will even quip that Yoo is actually from the Unified Silla period (668–935), an era that didn't have a culture of seonbi. This is not to say that Yoo is overly serious or without a sense of humor—rather, whether in his poems or love of sharpening pencils by hand—it's hard to tell what era he belongs to.

In translating Yoo's work, I've tried to honor his syntax and sense of play with the resonances of rhythm, sound, and image from the Korean whenever possible. He eschews conventional turns of phrase and finds minute linguistic opportunities to make the everyday strange.

In "peonies," another poem about romantic love, the speaker's curiosity about the object of a crush spreads and crawls with imaginative feeling and abandon underscored by not knowing and wanting to know. The speaker's thoughts and emotions "climb night and writhe into bloom." Rather than climbing at night, these imagined flowers climb night itself, perhaps to emphasize the intensity of feeling fueled by not knowing.

> the peonies you said you'd planted climb night
> and writhe into bloom, not knowing when these
> flowers are supposed to bloom and believing it is
> now summer, not knowing if you have a garden, and
> if not that, not knowing if you planted the peonies in
> a flowerpot or how the flowerpot glimmers brightly,
> not knowing anything

And even in the heat of this rhizomatic unfurling of desire, the poem is also self-aware of the vulnerability inherent to crushes: "those flowers, the peonies you said you'd planted, bloom and creep."

In "falling inside," the word for time is repeated and appears at the end of poetic phrases. The poem explores the circularity of time, memory, and mortality; for context, Yoo mentioned that this poem is based on a memory of visiting his father's grave, leaning against it after offering soju. In my translation, I've used anaphora at the beginning of the poetic phrases to prioritize the spell-like rhythm and repetition in the Korean and to preserve the sense of circularity and swirling.

> the time of the hairstreak butterfly flying away as a swallowtail butterfly, the time of sitting with my back turned, the time of the midday sun before its heat, the time of dust dividing and drifting away its numbers, the time of dandelion seeds floating up and sinking and floating again,

Similarly, I considered multiple options for the repeated introductory phrase in Yoo's debut poem that appears as the second poem in the collection, "when i put my neck inside a t-shirt i think." The original phrase in Korean isn't how someone would normally describe putting on a shirt, suggesting an awkwardness or laboriousness between garment and body beyond the automatic, everyday action of getting dressed. I tried "when i stick my neck inside a t-shirt i think" in an earlier version, but "stick" was too distracting. "when i put on a t-shirt" or "when i slip on a t-shirt" seemed not strange or unfamiliar enough for the job. And "when i slip a t-shirt around my neck" veered too close to literal gallows humor. Ultimately, I chose an option that allowed a strange door to open to multiple interpretations and images—a rabbit hole, a daily ritual, a meditation, a noose, a headspace for you to encounter yourself before heading out for the day.

In "empty frame," removing an old photograph from the wall after the father's passing reveals the absence left behind.

> the exposed wall is bright
> how did it happen
> that the days that were, are sadder
> than the days that won't be

For the speaker, the incomprehensibility of losing his father makes the times they spent together, all those memories, more devastating than the lost future. In the Korean, the poem ends with "are sadder"—in my translation I moved the phrase to end the previous stanza to emphasize the being and not being of their days together.

In the summer of 2022 and 2024, I had the opportunity to discuss my translations with Yoo at wit n cynical in Seoul. During both visits I witnessed firsthand his palpable influence within the literary community. Despite his widespread influence, Yoo's poetry has been unavailable in English translation beyond the individual pieces I've published in literary journals over the past several years.

It is also worth noting that the book's cover features a black-and-white photo taken by Yoo in November 2024. Yoo is an avid photographer with a soft spot for black-and-white analog techniques. As in his poetry, he's more interested in capturing the shadows than the light. Which again brings to mind Agamben's idea that "The contemporary is he who firmly holds his gaze on his own time so as to perceive not its light, but rather its darkness. . . . The contemporary is precisely the person who knows how to see this obscurity, who is able to write by dipping his pen in the obscurity of the present." Yoo is a poet who writes in the dark and in the obscurity of the everyday as a consummate contemporary.

When I asked Yoo about what he thought made his poems stand out, he named their quietness. In the cover photo, Yoo captures the quiet stillness of light entering the window of his bookshop. He had never seen the light like this before, and he felt that this play of light and shadow might never come to pass again. He shares the photo along with the greeting, "I wonder if I lived today just to take this photo."

—Stine An
April 2025
New York City

Sources

Agamben, Giorgio. "What Is the Contemporary?" In *What Is an Apparatus? and Other Essays*, translated by David Kishik and Stefan Pedatella, 39–54. Stanford, CA: Stanford University Press, 2009.

Anusual. "EP.01 시인 유희경" ["EP.01 Poet Yoo Heekyung"]. YouTube video, 4:42. Posted April 29, 2017. www.youtube.com/watch?v=cnUObTkKW2I.

Cho Jongyeop. "한쪽 눈 잃고 비로소 詩를 얻다" ["Losing Sight in One Eye, Gaining Poetry"]. 동아일보 [*The Dong-A Ilbo*], January 13, 2017. www.donga.com/news/Culture/article/all/20170113/82355038/1.

Cho Yeonjung. "해설: 최초의 감정" ["Commentary: Emergent Feelings"]. In 오늘 아침 단어 [*Today's Morning Vocabulary*], by Yoo Heekyung, 122–153. Seoul: Moonji Publishing, 2011.

프럼에이 [From A]. "젊은 예술, 문학을 만나다 Interview 9. 시인 유희경" ["Meeting Young Artists and Writers, Interview 9: Poet Yoo Heekyung"]. YouTube video, 6:59. Posted August 31, 2017. www.youtube.com/watch?v=cGJqeODVTAk.

Kwak, Youna. "Answering the Call: Beyond Resistance and Liberation." *Chicago Review* 64/65, no. 4/1 (2021): 100–113.

Lee Kuenhye. "'오늘 아침 단어' 공식 보도자료: 짐짓, 말하지 못했던 우리의 감정에 대해" ["Official Press Release for 'Today's Morning Vocabulary': On the Feelings We Left Unspoken"]. 문학과지성사 [Moonji Publishing], June 6, 2011. Press release. moonji.com/book/6140.

Lee Yunju. "포스트 미래파가 부르는 '사부곡'" ["A Post-Miraepa Poet Sings a 'Sabugok'"]. 주간한국 [*Hankook Weekly*], June 22, 2011. weekly.hankooki.com/news/articleView.html?idxno=4261079.

Lee Yunju. "시동인 '작란', '포스트 미래파' 대표주자" ["Poetry Collective Jaknan, Representatives of the 'Post-Miraepa' Movement"]. 주간한국 [*Hankook Weekly*], August 30, 2011. weekly.hankooki.com/news/articleView.html?idxno=4313201.

Song Yongchang. "포스트 미래파, 유희경 첫 시집 '오늘 아침 단어'" ["Post-Miraepa, Yoo Heekyung's First Poetry Collection 'Today's Morning Vocabulary'"]. 한국일보 [*Hankook Ilbo*], June 26, 2011. www.hankookilbo.com/News/Read/201106260984337835.

Acknowledgments

This book would not have been possible without the generosity and support of many individuals, communities, and institutions.

I am deeply grateful to the many institutions who provided support, including the National Endowment for the Arts, PEN/Heim Translation Fund Grant, American Literary Translators Association, the Corporation of Yaddo, and LTI Korea.

I would also like to thank all the publications who published earlier versions of the translations in this collection, especially: *Action Books Poetry in Action*, *Best Literary Translations* series, *Black Sun Lit*, *Chicago Review*, *The Southern Review*, *Waxwing*, and *World Literature Today*.

Special thanks to Christopher Mattison, Leora Zeitlin, J. Kates, and everyone at Zephyr Press for their careful attention, thoughtful feedback, and belief in this book. Your guidance has strengthened this work in immeasurable ways.

I am indebted to my mentors and peers in the poetry and literary translation communities. To Sawako Nakayasu, thank you for inviting me into literary translation—it's been a dream to learn how to say translation is art with you. To Don Mee Choi and Joyelle McSweeney, thank you for your generous mentorship and support in bringing *Today's Morning Vocabulary* into the world—your insights and guidance have shaped my approach to translation and have given me permission to explore translation as an anti-neocolonial mode and a zone for deformation. To Simone White, thank you for showing me that this is it.

A big thank you to the following individuals and communities who provided support, inspiration, and feedback over the past several years: Aaron Robertson, Alex Zucker, Anton Hur, Archana Madhavan, Barbara Ofosu-Somuah, Bruna Dantas Lobato, Chenxin Jiang, Darcie Dennigan, E. J. Koh, Emily Jungmin Yoon, Kim Hyesoon, Jack Jung, Jacob Rogers, Jacqui Cornetta, Jeffrey Zuckerman, Jenna Tang, Jennifer Shyue, Jeremy Tiang, Jimin Seo, Julia Sanches, Ju Ly Ban, Kate Hedeen, Katrine Øgaard Jensen, Kelsi Vanada, Kira Josefsson, Marci Calabretta Cancio-Bello, Madhu Kaza, May Huang, Mayada Ibrahim, Mónica de la Torre, Nicholas Glastonbury, and Soje; the BIPOC Literary Translators Caucus, the 2023 BCLT Summer School Korean Language Workshop, the Translation Across Disciplines conference at Brown University, chogwa zine, the League of Extraordinary (KOR–ENG) Translators: A Working Group, Us & Them, and wit n cynical.

Thank you to Hyunwoo Kim and Nasun Agency for their support and encouragement.

To Jein Han, thank you for reading early drafts, offering thoughtful critiques, and inviting me to collaborate on a workshop space where our vocabularies could root and flower. I'm so excited for our translations to meet the world together this year and can't wait for them to be in conversation.

To my family, especially my maternal grandparents, thank you for giving me a reason and urgency to hold on to the Korean language—it was because I wanted to hold on to your stories and lives and share my life with you. Mom and Dad, thank you for the countless KakaoTalk conversations and calls to discuss Korean poetry and help me write better emails in Korean.

To Yoo Heekyung, thank you for inviting me back into the Korean language and for entrusting me with your work. It's an honor to introduce your words into English. Thank you for your friendship, warmth, and support, and I'll always look forward to our conversations on poetry.

To Luke, my best friend and partner, thank you for bearing with me and for your unwavering support through this journey. I would not have completed this project without your unconditional love and belief in my work and person. Thank you for your wisdom, patience, and kindness.

Finally, this book is dedicated to Joachim Neugroschel and his beautiful and mysterious translations of Franz Kafka. His translations made me fall in love with literature and writing when I didn't know that I would become a writer and literary translator. I have carried his name and his translation of Kafka's "The Trees" with me ever since. Your work changed my life.

Contributor Biographies

Yoo Heekyung (b. 1980) is an acclaimed South Korean poet, playwright, and essayist. He is the author of more than ten collections of poetry and prose, including *Photography and Poetry* (Achimdal Books, 2024) and *Winter Night Rabbit Worries* (Hyundae Munhak, 2023). Yoo studied creative writing at the Seoul Institute of the Arts and playwriting at the Korea National University of Arts. He debuted as a poet in 2008 when his poem won the spring literary contest sponsored by the *Chosun Ilbo*. He is a playwright with the theater company *dock* and a member of the poetry collective *jaknan*. A recipient of Today's Young Artist Award (2023) from the South Korean Ministry of Culture and the Hyundae Munhak Literary Award (2020), Yoo lives in Seoul where he runs the poetry bookshop and project space wit n cynical.

Stine An is a poet, literary translator, and performer based in New York City. Her work has appeared in *Best Literary Translations 2024*, *Best American Experimental Writing 2018*, *Poem-a-Day*, *Words Without Borders*, *Electric Literature*, and elsewhere. She holds a BA in Literature from Harvard College and an MFA in Literary Arts from Brown University. She is the recipient of fellowships and grants from The Poetry Project, the PEN/Heim Translation Fund, Yaddo, ALTA, Vermont Studio Center, and the National Endowment for the Arts. Her publications include *S_MMER CR_SH* (Sarabande Books, 2025) and *Comet and Star* written by Lee Juck and illustrated by Lee Jinhee (Enchanted Lion Books, 2024). Her debut poetry collection, *B-Dragon Suite*, was a winner of the 2023 Nightboat Poetry Prize.